MaDea's Plantation

Cookbook

D1373338

Recipes from the Old South

Wise words about and for mothers

By Toni Mariani

Dedication Page

This book is dedicated to all the mothers in the world. And not only the mothers but all the women, because if you didn't have your own child, I am sure you mothered someone else's.

Raising children to be productive members of society is the most difficult job in the world, and the woman was designed to do it, along with her husband and Creator.

Feeding them is almost impossible without the help of others. Here's a bit of help.

I have been fortunate enough to know a lot of women in my family beginning with my great-grandmothers on both sides of the family. They have been godly women, those who keep seeking to know His truth, and I appreciate them.

So, to all mothers with love.

Contact information

https://www.amazon.com/author/tonimariani

https://www.goodreads.com/tonimariani

https://www.facebook.com/authortonimariani

https://www.CreateSpace.com/6983899

bware@sheboygan.k12.wi.us

Table of Contents

Title Page

Dedication Page

Contact Information

Table of Contents

Utensils needed

Breakfast dishes

Catfish & Grits

Shrimp & Grits

Hoecakes & Buttermilk

Ham & Eggs MaDea style (Omelet today)

Corn Muffins & Sweetenin, Fried eggs & Potatoes

Hoecakes & Peaches with cream

Rice, Scrambled eggs with peppers & onions

Scratch Biscuits, Sausage with gravy

Special Note

Remember that you are the one who knows your allergies and what your family can tolerate. Please feel free to substitute or leave out anything you feel is necessary. You can email me with questions, and I will help you find a solution. White/granulated sugars can be replaced with organic vanilla yogurt, or half honey and half brown sugar. Have fun and try different ways, according to taste. Mashed fruits can replace eggs. Just try those that won't change flavor.

Utensils needed

MaDea said you cannot cook without a cast iron skillet. She received hers as a gift from her Master (and adopted son) William Thompson Sr. She never measured because once she prepared a dish she never forgot how, she used to say. Please remember that MaDea had no modern tools that we can now grab and pick up out of the kitchen. No temperature thermometer's, no wire whisk, no plastic or nicely shaped metals but later in her life, she was able to use heavy iron tools. MaDea did not write things down, even if she knew how to later in her life, but taught her children what she knew by action, sharing her meals with them in love.

MaDea used expressions like "a pinch", "a dash", "little spoon", "big spoon", "a peek at", "right color", "look see", "give it time", "a dab", "eyeball it", and even "one or two handfuls".

Utensils

Pancake Turner

Whisk

Baking pans (MaDea used what was available)

Spatula

Large mixing bowl

Measuring cup/spoons

Teaspoon

 Large stirring spoon

Small mixing bowl

Large pot

Small pot

 (MaDea used an open fire)

Today a stove top and oven

Catfish and Grits

Clean fresh caught catfish, taking off the head, split down the middle, peel skin away, throw away all the insides.

Cut the two halves lengthwise again, so you have four filets.

Your cast iron skillet should be bubbling in hot oil; just enough to cover the fish, not drown the skillet.

Pour 2 cups of cornmeal in a large mixing bowl and add a ½ cup of flour. Stir the two together. Mix together 1 tablespoons of seasoned salt and pepper, 1 teaspoon of chopped dried red peppers, and 2 tablespoons of onion powder. Shake bag. Dump seasonings into cornmeal and flour, mix with spoon.

On a flat cookie sheet like pan, shake out bowl from top to bottom, spreading the full length of pan. Lay filets onto mixture, coating well, and flip over and coat other side. (Treat fish gently, and don't shake up in bag)

Carefully lay out in hot oil one piece at a time. Leave enough room to flip each one after browning. Use a grease splatter screen. (Dollar store item) After browning and crispy looking, lay out on paper towels just long enough to drain excess oil. If you like it spicy, shake hot sauce on filets. If you like lemon, dribble some on.

Grits are a food all unto themselves, made from corn, ground up into a coarse meal and them boiled. But, today's cooks just use grits out of a box or single packet. MaDea had to grind hers up in a grinder. Thank God we don't have to work that hard to get a quick meal.

Bring water to a boil. For each cup of grits, use 2 cups of water. Pour the grits into the pot. Add a tiny dash of seasoned salt, mix and stir. Watch and stir the whole time, simmering until thick enough for your taste. Top with butter and pepper to taste, or shredded cheese and pepper. Spoon out onto plate next to fish.

You have a child now and you can't be a perfectionist anymore!

Mary Beth Hurt

Shrimp and Grits

The grits you have learned how to make in the above recipe, so for the shrimp, first clean shrimp, deveining them. MaDea would have had to clean and peel them, but now they come in a bag frozen. I would get the deveined and peeled bag. Pot of water should be boiling first, then gently put shrimp in pot of hot water. Boil until white, or follow directions on bag. Season with butter and a dash of garlic powder, or add your favorite cheddar cheese, then spread across grits. Enjoy.

Hoecakes with Buttermilk

Hoecakes are just another term for cornbread cooked in a skillet like pancakes, and the difference is one uses cornmeal and the other uses flour. They called it hoecake because "po" folks, like the enslaved had to use whatever metal would heat up on an open flame, when they were cooking in their own homes. There were no stoves like up at the big house. In MaDea's day they ground the corn of into a meal, using the yellow dried kernels. Today it's already done for us, so just follow the directions on the bag for the amounts. One addition is to add 1 & ½ teaspoon of sugar for sweeter bread. Apply cooking spray or several teaspoons of oil, not as much as the fish to skillet. Don't get the oil as hot as you would when frying fish. Warm oil is good, and spoon round heaping spoonfuls of mix on the oil. When you see the top forming air bubbles, and the edges are getting brown, use a flat pancake turner and turn it over. You don't have to do any high flipping, just enough to turn it to the other side. I would do one at a time, so you can concentrate on each one. Then put each one on a plate and cover with foil. As you finish one, add it on top of the other, so they stay warm.

Crumble into a cold glass of buttermilk, and add a sprinkle sugar. Yum.

We called our maternal grandmother Big Mama.

Her name was LV.

When we were little girls we asked her,

"Big Mama, how do you spell LV?"

She said with an exasperated look and her hand on her hip,

"L. V.! When you say it, you spell it!" We all L O A O!

Ham and Eggs MaDea's Way

Beat 4-6 eggs in a small bowl. Add 2 tablespoons of cream or milk. Do not use anything but cow's milk. Cut up pieces of either cooked ham, bacon, sausage or any other meat already cooked. Cut a half an onion. MaDea did not have sweet onions, but we do today, so if you have one use that. Cut up a sweet pepper of your choice or use all of them; green, red, yellow and if you want to, add a sprinkle of chopped red peppers from a shaker. These are hot so just a dash. Get your skillet warm and add butter, oil spray, **_or_** bacon fat that you are saving in a cup in the refrigerator (MaDea's way). Just enough to coat the pan not like frying fish. (Smile) Don't spray near open fire. (MaDea would say unless you want to be bald) Lightly heat your onions and peppers and then add the beaten eggs to this. Then dump your chosen meat into this. Since you are not a genius at flipping like she was, MaDea would say either stir it all together, _or_ let the bottom set (stiffen a bit) and then fold it over in half and turn heat down and let it cook slowly for about 10 minutes, until the inside is cooked. (the heat should be _way_ down so it won't burn) Then turn it out onto a plate. Eat as a side, or a main dish.

Listen, my son, to the discipline of your father, and do not forsake the law of your mother.

Proverbs 1:8

Corn Muffins & Sweetenin/ Fried Eggs & Sliced Potatoes

For this recipe you can use the same corn muffin blend that you used before. Use a muffin pan, and add paper cups or, ***If you don't*** use paper cups, then prep the pan by this method: turn the oven setting to 425 and put a little oil in the bottom of each cup. And of course coat the inside of each cup of the pan and sit the empty pan in the oven until the oil heats up, about 3 minutes. Then take out and pour the batter in the pan. The pan is hot! Be careful! This method will curl the tops of the muffins inward to make a decorative look to the muffins. Once cups are filled, put back in oven and ***watch very*** carefully since the heat is higher than normal. When done, lightly butter each one and add a drop or two of molasses. This is the sweetenin. (if you want to you can use maple syrup.) Yum!

For the potato's, peel, wash and cut into small chunks. Peel an onion and cut into the same size chunks and stir together. MaDea liked to boil her potatoes for 10 minutes first to get that extra starch off, and drain. Then put in that iron skillet lightly coated with oil. Turn heat down once they are all in, and ***watch and turn*** every 6-10 minutes until done. You can add drops more of oil as needed until done, and a sprinkle of water to get them extra soft. If you rather they stay crispier, then don't add the water. Season to taste. (Don't use butter because it will burn)

Eggs are cracked into a lightly oil-coated skillet. Leave them set (hardened) on the bottom. Then take a tiny bit of hot oil and spoon over the tops of the eggs. This way you don't need to flip them. Wa-La!

Hoecakes & Peaches with cream

MaDea had to cook everything from scratch. But that just added to the love that went into her recipes. My *Big Mama* (LV) used to make these and we were licking the plates and begging for more.

In your large mixing bowl sift together all the dry ingredients.

In your other bowl, whisk eggs until blended well into one light color. Whisk in the milks. Whisk in the melted butter and vanilla.

In the dry ingredients bowl, make an indentation in the middle, and slowly pour wet ingredients in there. With your spatula, turn the wet into the dry smoothly. It should be lumpy when mixed together. Don't over stir. Using your iron skillet, heat up some oil to a warm heat. Spoon each cake into a round mound, about 1/3 cup full. If they need help, smooth them with your spatula. Cook in heat until bubbles form in batter on top, and edges are browning. Watch your heat temperature. Flip. When each is done, put on a plate and cover with foil or a bowl to keep heat in. Add butter to top of each one, and whatever other topping you like; whipped cream, syrup, fruit. Wash off fresh peaches. Cut in slices. Put a bit of warm cream over them, and enjoy.

Dry Ingredients

- Flour – 2 cups
- Baking Powder-2t
- Salt -1t
- Baking Soda-1t
- Sugar -2T

Wet Ingredients

Eggs -2

Buttermilk -1cup

Whole milk-1cup

Real Butter -1/4 cup

Vanilla Extract-1t

hoecakes

shine light on your's

Fathers do not be irritating your children, but go on bringing them up in the discipline and admonition of God.

Ephesians 6:4

Rice, Scrambled Eggs with green peppers & onion

There is a trick to good rice, according to MaDea. She would say you have to have two fires; one high heat and one low heat. But for today, we just turn down the heat and simmer. So, put 2 cups of rice in a pot. Cover rice with water up to an inch over it. Put on high heat, and bring to a boil. Once boiled, turn down on low heat to simmer. Add a ½ tsp of seasoning salt, give it a stir and recover pot and set timer for 15 minutes, but still watch it. If it begins to boil up lift pot off heat until bubbles go back down. This happens several times until heat cools down. (Seasoning salt uses less salt and more of the other spices)

Whisk 4 eggs in small bowl, add a dash of whatever spices and seasonings you like, and pepper to your taste. Cut up green pepper and onion into slivers and heat in a little butter on low heat until onions are translucent. Pour eggs over pepper and onions in skillet and stir together with spatula. Dump over rice when both are done.

Shine light on your perfect rice

God could not be everywhere, so he made mothers.

A Hebrew Proverb

Pork Sausage/ Creamy Buttermilk Gravy
Scratch Biscuits

MaDea said that there is nothing like scratch biscuits and gravy on a cold day. She said northerners might not think it gets cold in the south, but there were times that she saw snow.

Since MaDea had access to fresh pork sausage she shared recipe according to that. But today's women are trying to eat healthier, so you can replace pork sausage with any kind of ground meat you like. Turkey sausage with added spices works wonderfully. If your meat comes with spices, no need to add the ones in the recipe. Either way break meat up, about 1 pound into medium heated skillet with a bit of oil added to meat if it's normally dry like turkey is. Let meat brown all the way around, flipping over about 3 times, using cooking spoon, (MaDea liked to use the wooden spoon; you know the one that we got popped with.) Then pour in the milk. ½ is buttermilk and the other ½ whole milk.

Pour in 1/4 cup of flour. Stir slowly so you're not slopping mixture out of pan. Mix well with a continuous stir. Reduce heat to simmer. When thick enough for your taste, pour in a serving bowl. If gravy gets too thick, add a tablespoon of milk until you like the consistency. Pour according to taste over your biscuits, one at a time. Yummy!

Ingredients

1 pound ground meat (if using a dryer meat, add 1 Tbs of olive oil if you have it)

1 ½ tsp smoked salt or seasoned salt

½ tsp of smoked paprika, (optional) or ½ of cayenne pepper (optional)

1 tsp of black pepper

2 tsp of brown sugar

½ tsp of garlic

½ tsp of fennel seeds

A pinch of celery salt

½ tsp of dried oregano

1 tsp of sage

A pinch of red pepper flakes

A pinch of cloves (crushed)

¼ cup of flour

2 cups of buttermilk, 2 cups of whole milk

Any seasoning that you don't want, leave it out.

Ingredients for scratch biscuits

I'm gonna let you know a secret that MaDea left special instructions about. Shhhh! Make sure your ingredients come from cold storage, try and use cool ingredients, ok cooks? And this is biscuits, not a ham. Gentle hands will be appreciated by the dough. Haha. So, no twisting, pounding or smashing.

Self-rising all purpose flour -2 cups

½ tsp salt

2 tbsp of brown sugar (light)

1 cup of cold butter milk

¼ cup cold whipping cream

6 tbsp cold butter

2 tbsp of cold butter flavored shortening

Instructions

Preheat oven to 450 degrees

MaDea didn't have parchment paper, so perhaps she used a brown paper bag, I don't know. We now have it, so go on and use it.

Line a cookie sheet with it

Large mixing bowl, add dry ingredients with whisk; flour, salt and brown sugar.

Use your cheese grater, and grate (scrape) cold butter into dry bowl.

Grate or spoon shortening in and gently stir together.

Make the well into the middle of mix (like you did the hoecake mix)

Pour the blended buttermilk and cream into the well (center of the mix.) Gently mix all together. Lay down a plastic working mat, or wooden board and flour. Put dough out on mat or board. Flour everything, even hands. Keep it floured as you work the dough. Knead dough folding it over several times. Pat dough out about 1 inch thick. Flour your cookie cutter and cut out by pressing down gently, no twisting remember. Pinch center of biscuit, and bake for 10-14 minutes, depending on how hot your oven gets. So watch them. Brush tops with butter when done. Pour sausage and gravy mixture over biscuits. Yummy!

Dinners

Salsa chicken and rice

Cream of chicken and potatoes

Chicken pot pie

Chitterlings and hogmaws (Hog intestines and stomach)

Meatballs, Pasta with tomato sauce

Southern Chili

Red beans & rice

Gumbo

Fried Cabbage

Southern Fried Chicken

Meatloaf and mashed potatoes

Greens and Hamhocks

Lasagna

Plantation Beef Stew (use whatever meat, rabbit, opossum, etc)

Southern style Macaroni & Cheese

Pork ribs, loin or roast

Pork ribs, Loin or roast

These are so good y'all gonna want to slap yo mama! (Just kidding) You can get any size package but check with a meat thermometer after the first 2 hours, that meat has reached 150 degrees or higher. Put thermometer in the thickest part of the meat, read and take out. (Wipe thermometer off before you put aside to bring temp back down on thermometer)

 MaDea of course had fresh hog, but we will use a cut from the store. Get boneless if possible. A trick for better flavor is to use Rib Rub, and you can find that in the store. Rinse the meat and pat dry with a paper towel. Rub meat all over with the rib rub. Put prepared meat in plastic bag and let it sit over night in refrigerator, so seasons can be absorbed into meat. MaDea would have wrapped it in cloth and put it in the cold ground, cold storage cellar or into a well.

If you don't have time to let it sit over night, try and give it as much time as you can. Preheat oven to 200 degrees and wrap your meat in foil and put on a cookie sheet so juices won't spill out. Slow bake your ribs, or roast for 2 hours, and then test for readiness. Your meat thermometer should read 160 degrees at least. Give 30 more minutes if not quite to your taste. Lather with bar-b-que sauce, or a steak sauce. It's delicious either way. Yummy!

Be wise my son, and make my heart rejoice.

Proverbs 27:11

Salsa Chicken and Rice

The difficult part you have already learned and that's the rice. I usually keep a pot of rice cooked at all times, because it's a staple in most homes. Just put the rice in a container and put it in the fridge.

You can use whatever part of a chicken you and your family like. MaDea was always feeding someone so she used the whole chicken after cutting off the head and feet. But we can pick up fresh cut up chicken from any store. If you buy a whole chicken make sure there is no part of it tucked down inside the neck. Sometimes butchers tuck the liver, giblet and neck inside. Wash chicken, and pat dry.

Make a chicken rub with seasonings already used in other dishes like, sage, paprika, garlic powder, onion powder and seasoned salt, black pepper or white pepper. Don't buy garlic salt or onion salt because in today's world there is too much salt in all the premade, packaged foods, so use the powders. If you buy salt anything, get seasoned salt, because there is or should be less salt in it than the other spices. Rub the chicken all over with the rub, and then cut a lemon in half and stuff inside the chicken. Cut up a few pieces of butter and put that inside. Cut an onion up and stuff that in, or as much as you can get in. Pour olive oil or a good quality oil over the chicken. Place in a bag and put in fridge over night, if you can. If not, get a deep baking dish and rub it inside with oil. Not the good stuff, use vegetable oil for pots and pans. Place the chicken in middle of dish, and pour salsa over the chicken. Wrap the dish up tightly and put in preheated oven on 200, and bake for 2 hours. As we said before, MaDea did not have a meat thermometer, but checked doneness by sight and time. If you are using a thermometer, chicken should be at least 160 degrees. Check it for doneness and if it falls off bone, it's ready. Make sure there is no pink.

If you want to give it ten more minutes with foil off to brown a little and to warm the salsa, do so. Spoon the salsa chicken pieces over the prepared rice. Yummy!

Grandma's hands clapped in church on Sunday morning,
Grandma's hands played the tambourine so well
Grandma's hands use to issue out a warning,
She said, 'Billy don't ya run so face might fall on a piece of glass,
Might be snakes there in that grass,
Grandma's hands!

Bill Withers

Shine light on
your perfect rice

Cream of chicken and potatoes

Prepare this dish with the same chicken as above, **_but_** take out the lemon from inside the chicken. With the chicken prepped to the oil step, set it aside and in the same kind of baking dish as before, pour a half can of cream of chicken soup in it, and half a can of cream of celery soup in. Put the other half of each soup either together or separate in a plastic bag or dish and freeze for another meal. In the empty can add a half a can of water, and half a can of whole milk. Stir up with a spatula, trying to dissolve the lumps. Sprinkle with black pepper only. The chicken should have enough other seasonings already on it. Cut up 4 large potatoes, or the number for your family. First wash and peel of course. Put in the soup mixture. Cut up another onion and put in it also, and if you want carrots or turnips. Place chicken in center of dish, and wrap up well with foil. Bake in a preheated oven at 200 degrees for 2 hours. Take out and check for pinkness, (blood on inside) and if falling off bones, done. Take off foil, swipe top with butter to brown. Enjoy.

Mom is a tough friend. I know she is going be honest with me.

Robert Eldridge

Proverbs 7:4

"Say to wisdom, 'you are my sister' and call understanding, "my relative!"

Chicken Pot Pie

This dish uses the same chicken as above, and the same biscuit dough. The dough will be rolled out thinner than when making biscuits and large enough to cover the dish you will use or individual sized glass Pyrex baking bowls. You can also use the same cream of chicken and cream of celery soup mixtures, because that's all the gravy in pot pie is. So the differences are cut up vegetables into bite size pieces; carrots, potatoes, turnips if you like, broccoli and even cauliflower if you so choose; also peas or green beans.

Break up the chicken in bite sized pieces. Throw out bones and spoon soup blend mixture, vegetables raw, and chicken into glass dishes stirring them together, and leave a little space at top so that it won't boil over. Lay biscuit dough over the top of each filled dish. Set dishes on a cookie sheet for easy handling purposes. In a preheated oven at 325 degrees, bake dishes for 30 minutes, watching for crust to get nice and golden. (You're eyeballing crust to a golden color rather than so much by time) Enjoy!

Beloved ones, let us continue loving one another,

because love is from God,

and everyone who loves has been

born from God and knows God.

1 John 4:7

Mom is such a special word

The loveliest that I've ever heard

A toast to you

Above all the rest

Mom you're special

You're simply the best.

Chitterlings and Hogmaws

For this recipe, you must remember that the enslaved were given the scraps of the meat, not the prime pieces. Chitterlings (MaDea called them Chitlins) are the lining of the hog's intestines and hogmaws are the stomach of the hog and were eaten every time the big house killed and ate a hog. Nothing was wasted on the plantation and MaDea and her people found ways to cook and eat the parts of all animals, and were glad to get it!

You can find both at grocery stores. If you don't see them in the frozen meat cases, ask the butcher. The chitlins come in either 5 or 10 pound buckets. It will take **_time to thaw_**, so prepare them a day or two ahead of when you plan on serving them. Hogmaws should come also frozen; look in frozen meat case or ask the butcher. They are tough before cooking, and *they both have a fat lining, so peel the lining off* during washing first. The hogmaws can cook while you are cleaning the chitlins. In a large pot, at least 6 quarts, or depending how many you are going to make, judge for yourself. Put hogmaws in and cover with water. Don't fill pot full of water, but leave about an inch from the hogmaws. Bring dish to a boil over medium heat. Then turn down and simmer for an hour. Watch water and refill if it boils down. After the hour, throw in a strainer, drain and cut up into 2 inches pieces on cutting board. Put back into the pot and set aside until chitlins ready to be added.

Chitlins must be cleaned thoroughly. These are the lining of intestines, right?

Using one side of your sink, fill with hot soapy dish water, and pour the thawed chitlins in. In the other side, or in a large bucket or pail have clean rinse water. Take each thin strip and peel away the translucent fat lining away from the thicker meat. Dip several times in the soap water, making sure there are no brown clumps left behind. Then throw in clean rinse water. I would wash at least twice in soap water, and rinse again. They cannot be clean enough, right? Using the same pot as the hogmaws were cooked in, add the chitlins and fill with water, enough to cover and room for a good boil. Add chopped onion, shake or two from red pepper shaker, and 1 tsp of vinegar. Stir and boil, then turn down and simmer for 3-5 hour, adding water when it gets low. Pour in strainer and drain, and put in serving dish. Cut up into bit size pieces, using sharp knife and fork. Eat with rice or whatever side you like.

Ingredients for Chitterlings and Hogmaws

5 pounds of Chitterlings

1 pound of hogmaws

1 onion, chopped

1 tsp salt

1 tsp vinegar

1 tsp minced garlic (minced garlic comes in a little jar, ask clerk)

½ tsp of red pepper flakes

Cookware

1 large pot

1 cutting board

1 sharp knife

Fork

Mild dish soap

This is what you will see in the freezer case, the 10 lb bucket.

Use your large pot!

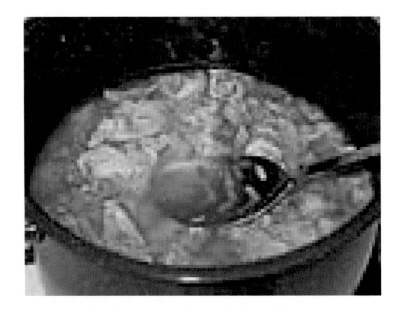

Add scallions and rammen noodles for variety.

Meatballs and Pasta with Tomato sauce

Pasta first- Boil half the pot of water, and add a teaspoon of salt. Throw in pasta, your favorite kind. Use a whole box for a family of at least 5. Let boil for 5 minutes. Then check to see if pasta is limp and soft. If not give it 5 more. Then drain and rinse in cold water.

Sauce-While that sits in strainer in sink, add garlic oil to the now empty pot, and add chopped onion, mushrooms, and minced garlic 2 tablespoons. Add fresh cilantro chopped up. Then add 2 fresh tomatoes chopped up, and 2 cans of tomato sauce. If not saucy enough, open a can of tomato paste and add that and a can of water. Stir up well and add drained pasta to sauce.

Meatballs-For the best flavor, choose several different ground meats. A 2 lb package of your favored should be large enough for a family of four (4), and a 1 lb package of the second choice. Beef, turkey, or Italian sausage will cook up wonderfully. Shape your choice of meats into round balls, keeping the meats separate since turkey stays white and is hard to tell when done if mixed. Sprinkle them with your favored seasonings, skipping salt. I use garlic powder, onion powder, Adobo seasoning which is found in the Latino recipes isle or a Latino specialty-cooking grocery store. It's a combination of herbs and spices. Read the labels and make sure salt is the least of the bunch, or none at all is best. If no salt is added, use seasoned salt in minute amounts. Using just enough oil in the bottom of your cast iron skillet, fry your meatballs until brown. Don't use olive oil to fry your meats, but you can add a few drops to the inside of the balls before frying for flavor; olive oil is one that doesn't react well to getting hot. Mix all together. Enjoy.

Southern Plantation Chili

Start with your big pot. If you want to make it just like MaDea used to, you have to soak your beans overnight. Half a bag of pinto beans, and half a bag of northern beans.

If you just have a few hours use canned beans. Let's pretend you don't have much time. Dump 1 can each of these beans: black, pinto, garbanzo, red kidney, light kidney, and northern in to your pot. Use the ground meat from the other recipes; beef, italian sausage, or turkey. I would use a combination, it makes for better flavor. Dump that in after you have already cooked it. Dump a can of any beer in. Dump in a can of stewed tomatoes and a can of diced tomatoes, preferably with either basil, green chili peppers or oregano in it. If the spices aren't in the can of tomatoes, put them in now. 1 tablespoon of each spice, with 3 tablespoons of chili powder, 3 tablespoons of cumin, 1 tsp of seasoned salt, 1 tbsp of black pepper and 3 tablespoons of minced garlic. If you have the whole fresh garlic, cut two sections from it, and chop up and add. If you want to, (MaDea couldn't of course) use prepackaged chili seasonings from the store. (If you do, you won't need to add the chili powder or cumin) Cook on medium heat for 10 minutes, then on simmer for 1 hour. Stir up every 15 minutes. Top with your favorites like sour cream and shredded cheese, or guacamole. Enjoy. For hotter chili, use red crushed peppers but only a ½ teaspoon.

Ingredients

1 can each of pinto, dark red kidney, light red kidney, garbanzo, black, northern,

2 pounds of cooked ground meat; either beef, turkey, italian sausage or a combination.

1 can beer

1 can of stewed tomatoes

1 can of diced tomatoes

1 tbs of oregano

1 tbs of seasoned salt

1 tbs of black pepper

1 tbs of cilantro

1 tbs basil

3 tbs of cumin

3 tbs of chili powder

2 sections from garlic clove, or 3 tbs of minced garlic

Toppings

Sometimes I add ¼ cup of red wine vinegar if you have it

Mamas don't let your babies grow up to be cowboys!

Various Singers

Red beans and Rice

Prepare rice as before. Set aside.

The day before you cook them, you will need **to wash** and sort through a whole bag of dried red kidney beans. You only need to use **warm water, and rinse**. Beans sometimes have rocks that look like beans in the bag, so look carefully. No one wants to bite down on one. Using clean water put them in your big pot with 2 bay leaves, a shake of red pepper, 1 tsp of garlic powder, 1 tsp of pepper, and 1 tsp of salt. Sit pot in fridge overnight. The next day, add a chopped onion. Bring beans to a boil, and then simmer for 2 hours.   To simmer means you cover with lid. After about an hour, make sure your water is still half way up over the beans. Stir. Then let them cook another hour and check the tenderness. You want your beans tender. When tender, soon out in a bowl over rice. Yum!

Gumbo

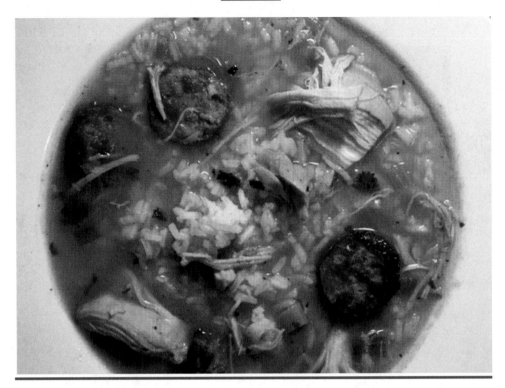

Prepare the rice as you learned how to. Set aside.

Use your big pot, six quarts.

Prepare your whole chicken as before, and cut out bones, _or_ boil chicken in this pot half filled with water, enough to cover chicken and (room for movement, MaDea would say) but about 4 cups of water. Put in a bouillon cube, and get a boil going, and then turn down on low for at least 90 minutes, or until meat falls off bones. Pull the rest off. Leave juices in pot, but go ahead and spoon out bones if you want. Add 2 cans of stewed tomatoes. Add in a cup of chopped up stalks of celery, shrimp prepared as you did before, and cut-up brats or spicy sausage. Add 1 chopped onion, and a prepackaged gumbo seasoning packet. Return this to low heat for at least 1 hour. Drain a can of corn and add, and also drain a can of peas and pour in. Add a bag of frozen okra to the mix. Add cooked rice for 10 minutes. Wa-la!

Ingredients

1 whole chicken (baked or boiled)

4 spicy sausages

1 bag of frozen shrimp (if you go shrimping have fresh)

1 bag of frozen okra

1 can of peas drained

1 can of corn drained

1 cup of chopped celery stalks

1 whole onion chopped

2 bouillon cubes

1 gumbo seasoning packet

2 cans of stewed or diced tomatoes

"M" is for the million things she gave me

"O" means only that she's growing old

"T" is for the tears she shed to save me

"H" is for her heart of purest gold

"E" is for her eyes with love-light shining

"R" means right, and right she'll always be.

Put them altogether, they spell "Mother"

A word that means the world to me.

Fried Cabbage

In your iron skillet, slow cook *4 pieces of bacon* or a medium size chunk of *fatback*. It makes it's own oil but if you need a bit add vegetable oil. Add a cut up *onion, (sweet)* and cook for about 10 minutes until translucent. Then add a whole cut up cabbage, which may seem like it won't fit but it should if you cut it up. Sprinkle with 1 tsp of *seasoned salt, pepper, Adobo seasonings* and *cayenne pepper* and pour ¼ cup of *water* over the cabbage. Don't let your cabbage dry out, but don't let it swim either.   Stir and cover, cook slowly on simmer until cabbage shrivels and softens. About 1 hour. Enjoy. We eat our dish with added brats grilled in oven on lowest setting for 30 minutes.

Southern Fried Chicken

This recipe makes chicken moist and delicious.

Prep the frozen chicken overnight by sitting it in a bowl of ice cold saltwater. 1 tsp of salt should be enough. Put in fridge. The second day put chicken in a bowl of butter milk and put it back in fridge, for a second day, pouring out the water.

We will start with one chicken and you can decide how many people will eat and get enough for them. MaDea would have cleaned the chicken, letting nothing go to waste. Today's cook can buy whatever part of the chicken she wants to use and not feel guilty about wasting any. The second day, take buttermilk soaked chicken and season with sage, seasoned salt, a sprinkle of chicken bouillon (yes it comes in a shaker) and black pepper. Flour each piece using your flour of choice, but I like wheat flour.

Using your cast iron skillet, pour half a skillet full of oil, about the same amount that you used for the catfish. Vegetable oil would be best. On medium heat, you should see tiny bubbles form on bottom when ready, but when hot gently place each piece in oil, starting with back of skillet. Cover bubbling chicken with a splatter screen. (get one from dollar store) Let cook until it is brown on each side, for about 25 minutes total, but turn every 6-10. To test for doneness, cut into a thick piece and no blood should come up. Or test with a meat thermometer to 160 degrees. (to test a piece, take out of the hot oil and put on a plate) Serve with vegetable and side dish like rice and gravy, pasta, your red beans and rice dish, etc.

Tupac Shakur wrote these words in a song to his mother:

Dear Mama,

You are appreciated.

I finally understand what it means for a woman to try and raise a man.

I see you come home after work late, trying to fix us a hot plate.

Don't ya know we love ya, sweet lady?

Meat Loaf and Mashed Potatoes

Ingredients

2 pounds of ground meat of your choice; turkey, beef, chicken, or for the best loaf, choice 1 pound each of two of them, and ¼ of italian ham. (ask butcher)

½ each of green pepper, red and orange

2 eggs

½ pack of saltines or ½ cup of bread crumbs crushed

½ onion, or more depending on taste

½ cup of portobello mushrooms or the kind you like

Preheated oven 300 degrees

Oiled baking pan or cookie sheet

¼ cup of worchestershire sauce

Chop up peppers, onions and mushrooms in either a bowl, or to save a step, into the baking dish directly. Crush the crackers or bread crumbs and add egg and worchestershire sauce. Mix in the meat. You can use your clean hands to mix all ingredients together, or use a wooden spoon. Shape the meat into a loaf or meat balls. Cover with foil and bake for an hour. Test with your meat thermometer if you want to. 160 degrees. You can top with a sauce (more worchestershire or A1, or ketchup) if you'd like to.

Mashed potatoes-wash 4 or 5 large potatoes, peel skin away. Boil until soft, drain away water, and mash up in a bowl. Add butter, pepper and a sprinkle of chives and seasoned salt.

Greens and Hamhocks

Today's cook buys her greens from the grocery store, but in MaDea's day the cooks grew and picked from their own gardens. Some greens were the tops of root vegetables that were thrown out, but remember the enslaved people found ways to eat the throw away food left from their masters tables. There are a variety of greens: collard, mustard, turnips, etc. These three are best cooked. Greens are best when the stalk and veins (ribs) of the leaf are broken away from the leafy part and thrown out.

Over your sink, break up greens and wash. Using your big pot, put the smoked hamhocks which are the ankles from the pig in and fill with water half way. Cut up an onion and throw in, along with 2 bouillon cubes. (I usually use chicken only for cooking) Pile the greens on top of the hocks and smash then down. Sprinkle tops of greens with your favorite spices and seasonings. Cover and cook over medium heat for about 2 hours, checking regularly, stirring until greens are limp and wilted down inside pot . Taste. Eat with corn bread and another side.

Ingredients

2 nice sized smoked ham hocks-used mostly for flavoring

4 bags of fresh greens-these will cook way down

1 onion

2 chicken bouillon cubes

Dash of black pepper, red pepper, seasoned salt, taste and add to your likeing.

Hocks are part of the pigs lower leg or ankle. You can use a nice piece of pork in place of the hocks.

Lasagna

This is my favorite pasta dish. I cook with dry pasta noodles. Cook your meat first in your cast iron skillet. I love mixing meats; it gives everything better flavor. So, if you need 2 pounds half should be one kind and half another. (I like beef and italian sausage) Fry up meat after spraying skillet lightly with oil. While cooking throw in a chopped up onion. (half) Brown meats. Drain. Mix in 2 cans of tomato sauce, and make sure it is saucy. Take your baking pan and spray it with oil all around evenly. Spread your meat sauce in a thin layer, and add the pasta noodles on top in a layer. Spread a layer of mozzarella cheese on that layer, and add a layer of cottage cheese on top of that, and shredded cheeses on top of that, and repeat until you get to the top and make the top layer the meat sauce. Cover dish with foil and bake in a preheated oven on 275 degrees for an hour. Check with a knife the doneness of the noodles. They should be soft all the way to the bottom. When done sprinkle with your favorite cheese.

There never was a child so lovely, but his mother was glad to get him to sleep!

Ralph Waldo Emerson

Plantation Beef Stew

Ingredients

Season beef cubes, about 2 pounds the night before with garlic powder and onion powder, and black pepper and 1 tsp of seasoned salt. Put in bag and refrigerate over night.

The next day, using your big pot, brown meat, on med high heat in 2 tsp of olive oil. Stir up, and try and keep meat apart. Set timer for 5 minutes for each side, and turn after 5 minutes each side. To pan, add cut up onion, one whole cut in cubes, adding a dribble of more olive oil as needed, and cook until translucent.

Pour in beef stock, unsalted, 2 ½ cups. Or you can use store bought unsalted chicken stock or vegetable stock.

Add in a bay leaf, garlic (2 tsp of minced) ½ tsp of Thyme.

Add 1 cup of chopped potatoes, carrots, and celery, each. I like to add portobello mushrooms. Bring to boil, then simmer for 2 hours, covered up.

Flour mixture is a cup of flour and ½ cup of stock. Stir together, and pour mixture into meat and veggies, and stir up. Bring to a boil, and then turn down for about 5 or 10 minutes. Pull out bay leaf, never eat that. Wa-la.

Your success as a family and our success as a society depends not on what happens at the White House, but on what happens inside your house!

Barbara Bush

The mother poems let mom know what a huge influence she has been in making you the person you are.

Why not give her a call today.

Toni Mariani

Southern style Macaroni & cheese

Ingredients

1 large bag of macaroni noddles
1 egg
1 stick of butter
1 cup of whole milk
¾ cups of sour cream
2 Tbs of sugar
½ tsp of salt
1 Tbs of black pepper
1 cup of sharp cheddar cheese
1 cup of mild cheddar cheese
1 cup of crushed bread crumbs or prepackaged cereal crumbs
½ block of velveeta cheese
1 cup of your choice of cheese (maybe the shredded mexican)

Using your big pot and baking dish, first cook the pasta for about 3 minutes in boiling salted water, because it will soften while baking. Drain water off in strainer. Dump in baking dish. Add milk, egg, sour cream, chopped up cheeses, sugar and butter. Mix up well.   Sprinkle your salt and pepper over top of dish last. Cover with foil, and bake in preheated oven for 1 hour at 275 degrees. Take out, add your shredded cheese, bread or cereal crumbs to top, return to oven to brown in broiler for about 1 or 2 extra minutes, watching all the time, with setting on broil. _Stay near and watch._ Delicious!

Say What!?

Families today seem to be even busier than ever before; always in a hurry and that's ok, because you can prepare delicious meals, store them all in individual freezer bags overnight, and put in the fridge to thaw while you are away during the day. Never leave food out on the countertops to thaw. Sit in the refrigerator.

When you get home, put in oven-safe baking dishes and warm in the oven on low, or microwave.

You still give your family the benefits of a home cooked meal with no guilt. You are cutting out extra salts and sugars in most pre-packaged meals, and that is the most important point.

Each day scientist come up with something new to add to ingredients in our foods, and most of them are not good. It is up to the parents, especially the mothers to weed out harmful products that might make it onto our family's dinner tables. We want to eat healthy foods, not those loaded with chemicals made in the laboratory.

Toni Mariani

Desserts

Cracker Candy

Strawberry Cheesecake

Southern Banana Pudding

Plantation Apple Pie

Big Mama's 7-Up Cake

Southern Peach Cobbler

Glazed Donuts

Dark Chocolate Candycane Brownies

White Chocolate-chip Cookies

Cracker Candy

Ingredients

1 tube of saltine crackers

1 cup of chopped nuts (any kind)

1 bag of chocolate pieces or 2 ½ bars

½ cup of coconut (my favorite addition)

Cookie sheet

Sheet of foil

Cooking spray

2 sticks of butter

 1 cup & 2 Tbs of Brown sugar

Line cookie sheet with the foil. Spray with the cooking spray. Lay out crackers side by side all over pan. Heat butter and brown sugar together in small pot at low boil for 3 minutes. Pour slowly over crackers. Smooth out with a spatula. Bake in preheated oven on 350 degrees for 3 minutes. This congeals it together. Add chocolate and spread out. Add nuts and coconut, and freeze for 20 minutes. Take out and break up, and serve. Delicious!

Cracker Candy

shine light on

your cheese cake

Strawberry Cheesecake

Ingredients for the Crust

Graham crackers-7 or 8

Melted butter-3 Tbs

For the Filling

Cream cheese-4, 8oz packages

Sour cream-1 cup

Sugar-1 ½ cups

All purpose flour sifted-1/4 cup

Whole milk-3/4 cup

Real vanilla-1 Tbs

Eggs-4

Preheat oven on 350 degrees.

This recipe makes use of a heavily buttered 9 inch spring form pan. Take 7 or 8 whole graham crackers. You can use a cutting board and crush them, or blend up in a food processor. Mix the butter in with crackers.

Press crackers mix into the bottom of pan, mashing down with a heavy glass. Work into sides of pan bottom about one inch high.

In your large bowl mix cream cheese with sugar until smooth. Blend in milk and eggs one at a time. Add in sour cream, vanilla, flour until smooth. Pour over crumb crust.

Bake in oven for 1 hour. Turn oven off and let cheesecake sit and cool inside oven. Give it 4-6 hours. Then put in fridge and let cool completely. Add your strawberry topping, or any other topping you'd like. Enjoy!

Southern Banana Pudding

Most cooks of today take the easy route when making banana pudding and use instant pudding. The plantation way was to make pudding from scratch using whole milk. Use a round glass dish when baking, or 8x8 foil pan.

1- Crack eggs and separate egg whites from yolks into separate bowls. Use 6 egg whites and 3 yolks.

2- Take an all natural vanilla bean, cut in half, and cut down the middle and take out black powder inside. Discard powder. Save bean shell.

3- In small pot, pour 1 ¾ cups of milk. Add sugar, 2/3 cup over low heat. Add 1 Tablespoon of vanilla extract, and vanilla bean. Mix together until milk is hot, on low heat.

4- In a separate bowl mix together 1 Tb of corn starch and 2/3 cup of milk mixture. Continue slowly stirring. Add to hot milk mixture on stove, and bring to simmer for 2 minutes. Turn off heat.

5- Lay a damp cold towel on counter, and sit bowl with yolks on top of it, and whisk together egg yolks and milk mixture in intervals, while stirring with whisk the whole time.

6- Put all back over stove, until it thickens. Don't let it boil, just thicken on low heat. Drain in a bowl with strainer, picking out the vanilla bean husk. Add 3 drops of your yellow food coloring and mix until well combined. Press plastic wrap down onto custard so you won't get film on top of custard. Put in fridge, covering with plastic wrap. Let sit for 45 minutes. This lets flavors blend and custard chill. Go ahead and clean up.

7- Make meringue, by blending egg whites, making peaks. Add 2 tsp of vanilla extract, and 2/3 cups of sugar, blending for about 35 seconds well. Add 1 & 1/2 tsp of cream of tarter. Blend with blender.

8- Press vanilla wafers into bottom of pan. Then cut up 2 bananas, each less than an inch thick, layer over wafers, and then layer custard onto bananas, and layer dish this way to the top; custard, bananas and vanilla wafers. And make sure you line cookies up on side also. Custard should be on top layer, then add meringue by spoonfuls or piping bag. Spread all around top. To brown the meringue peaks, put in 370 degree oven, put in broiler for just 25-35 seconds, watching so it won't over brown. You're just browning the peaks.

9- Put in fridge to chill for several hours, before serving. Delicious.

Ingredients

6 bananas at peak

Vanilla wafers, use Jacks or Nilla Wafers

For custard and meringue

Whole milk

Eggs

Pure vanilla extract

Corn starch

Cream of tarter

Yellow food coloring

9 inch glass dish or 8x8 pan

Vanilla beans (expensive, but best)

Plantation Apple Pie

Ingredients

Filling

Sugar ¾ cup

9-10 Apples (at least 2 kinds, one being Granny Smiths)

2 Tbs Lemon juice

¼ cup Corn starch

1 tsp Vanilla

½ tsp Allspice

1 tsp Cinnamon

Salt-a dash only

A bit of apple juice(1/4 cup)

Peel apples ahead of time cutting them into bit size chunks or chips and set aside in cool water. Mix all dry ingredients together in your large bowl, stirring with spoon. In small bowl mix apple juice, lemon juice and vanilla. Drain water off apples and put them in a large bowl. Pour wet ingredients over apples. Blend. Spoon apples and ingredients into your bottom crust inside your baking dish. Fill. Wet your finger, and tap your pie crust edges, so top crust will stick to bottom edges nicely. Crimp edges together to seal, tucking and waving top crust edges. With a knife, slit a few air holes in top. Melt butter and brush top and edges. Sprinkle a bit of sugar on top. Bake in preheated oven on 425 degrees for 15 minutes first, them take out to cover edges with foil so they won't brown unevenly from rest of pie. Reduce heat to 375 degrees, and bake for additional 45-55 minutes. Watch after 35 for a golden brown color.

Enjoy after cooling a bit, with your favorite topping; ice cream, caramel drizzle, etc.

The Crust

All purpose flour 3 cups

Salt 1 Tbs

1 egg

Milk 1 cup

Sugar 2 Tbs

1 Tbs lemon juice

½ cup each Lard & Crisco oil

In your large bowl, dump flour and salt, sugar and cut in crisco oil chunks and lard. Don't over work it, you want it flaky. Add egg and milk to equal 1 cup. Blend together with flour. Add the lemon juice. (if you have vinegar instead of lemon juice you can use that)

Flour counter top, sprinkling lightly. Throw flour mix out on counter and sprinkle in flour and let it sit to rest for 5 or 10 minutes. This amount will make a bottom and top crust. Add flour to hands. Pat dough out and flour rolling pin. Lightly roll out dough making sure to roll pin in all directions. Make sure you have even thickness all around. Then flour roller again, and roll dough around rolling pin to grab it and place over baking pan. Gently unroll. If crust hangs over edge of pan, lift and pinch your edges to make waves. Do the same for the top crust. Wa-La!

To store pie dough, if you are not planning on using it now, use parchment paper and wrap crust and paper around roller. Store in plastic wrap and baggie and freeze.

Did you know that sometimes the poorest women leave their children the richest inheritances?

Ruth E. Renkel

Big Mama's 7-up cake

Big Mama (LV) was famous for making a cake called the 7-up cake. It was mixed up and pour into a pan like this shape, called a bundt pan. I will duplicate her recipe below. My mother loved to make them for us and share at parties. It's smooth and rich.

Ingredients

A bundt cake pan

1 cup unsalted soft butter

½ cup butter–flavored shortening

3 cups white sugar

5 large eggs, room temperature

1 tsp vanilla extract pure

1tsp lemon extract

Zest of lemon (peelings scraped off. You won't need much)

Zest of lime (peelings scraped off. You won't need much)

3 cups of sifted all purpose flour

½ tsp of salt

¼ cup of heavy whipping cream

1 cup of 7-up soda

7-up glaze (make this by combining 1 cup of powdered sugar and 2 tablespoons of 7-up soda)

Instructions

Preheat oven to 325 degrees. Grease and flour your bundt pan.
In a large mixing bowl cream together butter, shortening, and sugar. Mix in eggs one at a time. Fold in the lemon and vanilla extracts. Fold in the pieces of lemon scrapings and lime scrapings called zest. Add in the flour and salt and mix well. Add in heavy cream and 7-up and mix well. Spoon batter into bundt pan. Bake for 1 hour and 5-15 minutes, watching it and checking with toothpick for doneness. Let sit, until cake has cooled enough so that icing won't run right off, but will stick nicely. Then turn out onto cooling rack or plate, and drizzle with glaze. You will love it's moistness. Enjoy.

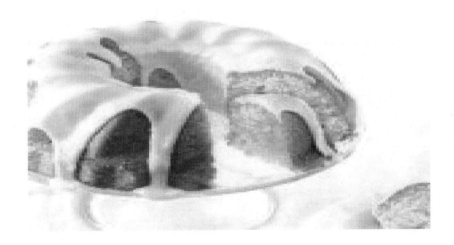

A stupid son brings adversity on his father, and a quarrelsome wife is like a roof that never stops leaking!

A house and wealth are inherited from fathers, but a discreet wife is from God!

Proverbs 19:13, 14

Southern Peach Cobbler

Ingredients

½ cup of melted butter

1 can of sliced peaches, drain(15 ¼ oz can)

Or 10 whole peaches cut up in bite size chunks

1 & 1/4 cups of sugar, divide in half

1 cup of all purpose flour

1 cup of milk

2 teaspoons of baking powder

¼ tsp of salt

1/8 tsp nutmeg

¼ tsp ground cinammon

You know your family's allergies, so leave out or substitute anything you need to. You can play with recipe by replacing ½ the white sugar with brown, or substitute organic vanilla yogurt for the white sugar. Try several different ways, we do!

Today's cooks might choose to use can peaches to save time, but the plantation way, was to pick peaches, clean and peel.

Pour butter into shallow baking dish, and set aside. Drain peaches, holding back a ¼ cup of the juice. (If you use fresh peaches, mix them with a little a little water and tiny bit of lemon juice, and then do the next step) In a small pan, bring peaches and juice to a low boil and stop. Take off heat. In a small bowl mix together sugar, flour, milk, baking powder and salt, and mix well. Pour this all over the butter in dish. Spoon peaches over batter, and sprinkle with remaining sugar. Bake at 400 degrees in preheated oven, for 25 minutes or until sticking a toothpick in it and it comes out clean. Serve warm. Yummy!

Glazed Donuts

Ingredients

2 packages of yeast (1/4 oz size)

¼ cup of water (warmed)

1 ½ cups of milk heated, then cooled

½ cup of white sugar

1 tsp of salt

2 eggs

½ cup of shortening or coconut oil

5 cups of all purpose flour

Vegetable oil

Creamy glaze, or you can use the glaze you put on the 7up cake.

1/3 cup butter

2 cups of powdered sugar

1 & 1/2 tsp of vanilla

4-6 tablespoons of hot water

Using a large mixing bowl dissolve yeast in warm water. Add milk, sugar, salt, eggs, shortening and 2 cups of the flour. Mix on low for 30 seconds, scraping bowl with spatula the whole time. Then turn mixer to medium level for 2 minutes, scraping bowl with spatula to keep all mix blended.

Add in remaining flour. Mix smooth. Cover with towel and let dough rise, about an hour. Then dump out on floured counter, or a plastic work mat. Roll on mat and coat with flour. Roll it out ½ inch thick with floured rolling pin. Cut with floured doughnut cutter. Cover these, and let them rise, about 30-40 minutes. Heat vegetable oil in your large pot or deep fryer if you have one. Madea did not have an electric one of course.

Slide the donuts into the oil carefully. You can use a metal wide spatula. As they heat they will bounce to surface, then turn. When golden brown, about 1 minute on each side, remove and cool.

Dip or squeeze glaze on each and cool. Yum.

To make the creamy glaze, heat butter until melted and remove from heat. Stir in powdered sugar and vanilla until smooth. Add water, bit by bit until you get the consistency you want.

Mama, the lady who birthed me when she was still a young girl herself,

Mama, she delivered me sick, but loved me none the less.

Mama, she was there when I fell down and scrapped my knee,

Mama, she held me when that first boy pulled my braids.

Mama, held me again when that same boy asked me to become his wife,

Mama walked me down the aisle when my father went away.

Mama was there to hold my hands while I pushed out my own child.

Mama, now that you are older and need me, I am here to hold your hand, and I have become your

Mama!

Toni Mariani

Dark Chocolate Candy Cane Brownies

Ingredients

¾ cup of dark chocolate

1 cup of white sugar

1/3 cup of butter cut in chunks

2 Tbs water

2 large eggs

1 tsp of pure vanilla extract

¾ cup of all purpose flour

¼ tsp of salt

1 cup of candy cane pieces

Preheat oven to 325 degrees. Line an 8 inch square baking pan with foil and lightly grease.

In a small saucepan, heat dark chocolate, sugar, butter and water over low heat stirring constantly until all melted together. Pour into medium sized bowl, and add eggs, whisking until well blended. Stir in vanilla, and add flour and salt, stirring well. Stir in candy cane pieces, and pour into baking pan. Sprinkle what's left of the candy cane pieces over mixture.

Bake for 42-45 minutes, or until a toothpick stuck in center, comes out slightly sticky. Cool completely in pan on wire rack. Then, lift out of pan by foil edges onto cutting board. Cut and remove foil, and store them in tightly covered container. Should make 16 brownies.